First Facts®

The Middle Ages

The Medieval Plague

by Sheri Johnson

Consultant:
James Masschaele
Associate Professor of Medieval History
Rutgers University
New Brunswick, New Jersey

Capstone
press®

Mankato, Minnesota

First Facts is published by Capstone Press,
151 Good Counsel Drive, P.O. Box 669, Mankato, Minnesota 56002.
www.capstonepress.com

Books published by Capstone Press are manufactured with paper
containing at least 10 percent post-consumer waste.

Library of Congress Cataloging-in-Publication Data
Johnson, Sheri.
    The medieval plague / by Sheri Johnson.
    p. cm. — (First facts. The Middle Ages)
    Summary: "Describes the spread of the plague during the Middle Ages, including its
symptoms and the effects it had on history" — Provided by publisher.
    Includes bibliographical references and index.
    ISBN 978-1-4296-3334-5 (library binding)
    1. Plague — History — Juvenile literature. 2. Diseases and history — Juvenile
literature. 3. Black Death — Juvenile literature. I. Title. II. Series.
RC172.J646 2010
614.5'732 — dc22   2009005060

Editorial Credits
Megan Schoeneberger, editor; Kim Brown, set designer; Matt Bruning, book designer;
    Svetlana Zhurkin, media researcher

Photo Credits
Corbis/Bettmann, 10; The Granger Collection, New York, 13; Mary Evans Picture
Library, 1, 5, 14 (left), 14–15, 19 (right), 20; North Wind Picture Archives, 6, 9 (right); Peter
Arnold/Wildlife, 8–9; Private Collection/Look and Learn/The Bridgeman Art Library,
17; Shutterstock/Michael Taylor, 18–19; Shutterstock/Noam Armonn, cover (skull);
Shutterstock/Oleg Kozlov & Sophy Kozlova, cover (rat)

Essential content terms are **bold** and are defined at the bottom of the page where
they first appear.

Table of Contents

End of the World

What would the end of the world be like? In **medieval** times, people living in Europe thought the end had come. Why? Because of the deadliest **plague** of all time. The Black Death killed millions of people from 1347–1352.

∼∼∼∼∼∼∼∼∼∼∼∼∼∼∼∼∼∼∼∼

medieval — to do with the Middle Ages
plague — a very serious disease that spreads quickly to many people and often causes death

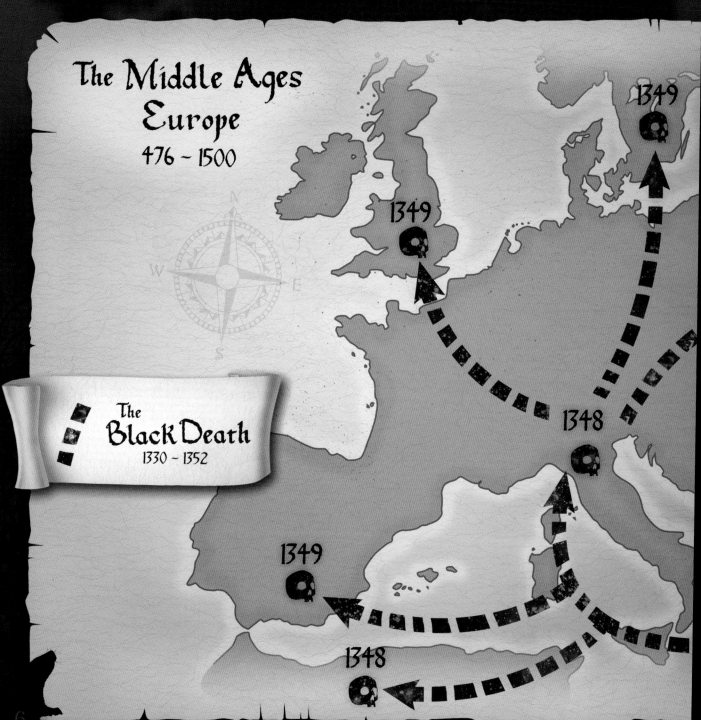

The Middle Ages
Europe
476 ~ 1500

The
Black Death
1330 ~ 1352

1349

1349

1349

1348

1348

1348

The Deadly Path

The Black Death started in Asia and moved across land and water. It spread to nearly every major city in Europe and reached Russia. How did the Black Death spread? Black rats and their fleas!

1352

From Asia - 1330

Flea Vomit

Black rats carried the germs that caused the Black Death. Fleas bit and drank the blood of the black rats. Later, these fleas bit people. While biting, a flea would **vomit** out the germs. The germs would then **infect** people.

vomit — to throw up
infect — to cause disease

The Plague at Sea

Sometimes the entire crew of a ship died from the plague while at sea. The ship would drift until it sank, met another ship, or landed on the coast.

Suffering

Once infected, a person began to swell. **Glands** in the neck and armpits got as big as apples. Dark spots formed on the skin. Blood and pus oozed out. Sometimes the glands burst open under the skin. Most plague victims died within three days.

gland — an organ in the body that makes natural chemicals or helps substances leave the body

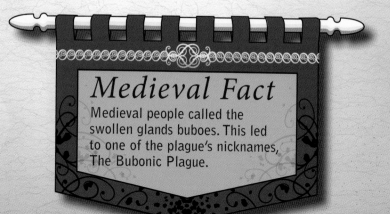

Medieval Fact

Medieval people called the swollen glands buboes. This led to one of the plague's nicknames, The Bubonic Plague.

Medieval Cures

Doctors did not know how to treat the plague. Sometimes they cut patients to make them bleed. They also pierced swollen glands. These painful treatments did not help plague victims.

The Blame Game

People in the Middle Ages could only guess what caused the Black Death. Many people thought it was caused by breathing stinky air. Some people blamed volcanoes and earthquakes. Others believed they were being punished by God.

Medieval drawing of a volcano

Stay Away, Plague!

Medieval people did not know how to prevent the Black Death. They tried to avoid the disease by wearing masks. They also tried carrying flowers, ringing church bells, and praying.

Black Death Count

The Black Death killed about 25 million people in only five years. Nearly one out of every three people died.

The plague did not go away. It came back many times over the next hundreds of years. But there were fewer victims.

Medieval Fact

There were not enough coffins to bury the dead. Instead, many bodies were buried in large group graves.

Finding the Cure

In 1894 scientist Alexandre Yersin found the germ that caused the disease. His discovery helped doctors treat plague victims.

People can still get the plague. Each year, between 10 and 50 people in the United States get the plague. But today the disease is easily treated with medicine.

plague germs

Alexandre Yersin

Medieval Fact

In the western United States, some prairie dogs carry the plague.

Amazing but True!

Pope Clement VI led the Roman Catholic Church during the Black Plague. His doctors told him to breathe pure air to stay healthy. They suggested surrounding himself with fire to cleanse the air. It was a lucky guess. They didn't know then that the plague germ was killed by heat. Pope Clement VI didn't get the plague.

Pope Clement VI

Try It Out: Travel Ban

To stop the plague from spreading, some towns would ban people from traveling. People could not enter or leave the city. Pretend you live in a town trying to keep out the plague. Make a poster that explains the rules of the travel ban. Why is the ban in place? How long will the ban last?

Glossary

gland (GLAND) — an organ in the body that makes natural chemicals or helps substances leave the body

infect (in-FEKT) — to cause disease by introducing germs or viruses

medieval (mee-DEE-vuhl) — having to do with the period of history between AD 500 and 1450

plague (PLAYG) — a very serious disease that spreads quickly to many people and often causes death

vomit (VOM-it) — to throw up food and liquid from your stomach through your mouth

Read More

Elliott, Lynne. *Medieval Medicine and the Plague.* The Medieval World. New York: Crabtree, 2006.

Macdonald, Fiona. *The Plague and Medicine in the Middle Ages.* World Almanac Library of the Middle Ages. Milwaukee: World Almanac Library, 2006.

Whiting, Jim. *Bubonic Plague.* A Robbie Reader. Natural Disasters. Hockessin, Del.: Mitchell Lane, 2007.

Internet Sites

FactHound offers a safe, fun way to find Internet sites related to this book. All of the sites on FactHound have been researched by our staff.

Here's all you do:

Visit *www.facthound.com*

FactHound will fetch the best sites for you!

Index